S0-DQV-872

NO LONGER PROPERTY OF
SEATTLE PUBLIC LIBRARY

CELEBRATING U.S. HOLIDAYS

Why Do We Celebrate
PRESIDENTS' DAY?

Patty Swinton

PowerKiDS
press.

New York

Published in 2019 by The Rosen Publishing Group, Inc.
29 East 21st Street, New York, NY 10010

Copyright © 2019 by The Rosen Publishing Group, Inc.

All rights reserved. No part of this book may be reproduced in any form without permission in writing from the publisher, except by a reviewer.

First Edition

Editor: Brianna Battista
Book Design: Reann Nye

Photo Credits: Cover Alex Pix/Shutterstock.com; p. 5 Ariel Skelley/DigitalVision/Getty Images; p. 6 wavebreakmedia/Shutterstock.com; p. 9 Miljan Mladenovic/Shutterstock.com; p. 10 https://en.wikipedia.org/wiki/File:Gilbert_Stuart_Williamstown_Portrait_of_George_Washington.jpg; p 13 Pigprox/Shutterstock.com; p. 14 Everett Historical/Shutterstock.com; p. 17 DavidNNP/Shutterstock.com; p. 18 Shu-Hung Liu/Shutterstock.com; p. 21 Courtesy of the Library of Congress; p. 22 KidStock/Blend Images/Getty Images.

Cataloging-in-Publication Data

Names: Swinton, Patty.
Title: Why do we celebrate Presidents' Day? / Patty Swinton.
Description: New York : PowerKids Press, 2019. | Series: Celebrating U.S. holidays | Includes index.
Identifiers: LCCN ISBN 9781508166658 (pbk.) | ISBN 9781508166634 (library bound) | ISBN 9781508166665 (6 pack)
Subjects: LCSH: Presidents' Day–Juvenile literature. | Presidents–United States–History–Juvenile literature.
Classification: LCC E176.8 S95 2019 | DDC 394.261–dc23

Manufactured in the United States of America

CPSIA Compliance Information: Batch #CS18PK: For Further Information contact Rosen Publishing, New York, New York at 1-800-237-9932

CONTENTS

Presidents' Day is the third Monday in February.

5

6

Presidents' Day is a day to learn about American Presidents.

The president lives and works in the **White House**. It is in Washington, D.C.

9

10

George Washington was our first president. He was born on February 22, 1732.

The **Washington Monument** honors George Washington. It is the tallest building in Washington, D.C.

13

14

Presidents' Day also honors Abraham Lincoln. Lincoln was born on February 12, 1809.

The **Lincoln Memorial** is also in Washington, D.C. Lincoln was America's tallest president.

IN THIS TEMPLE
AS IN THE HEARTS OF THE PEOPLE
FOR WHOM HE SAVED THE UNION
THE MEMORY OF ABRAHAM LINCOLN
IS ENSHRINED FOREVER

17

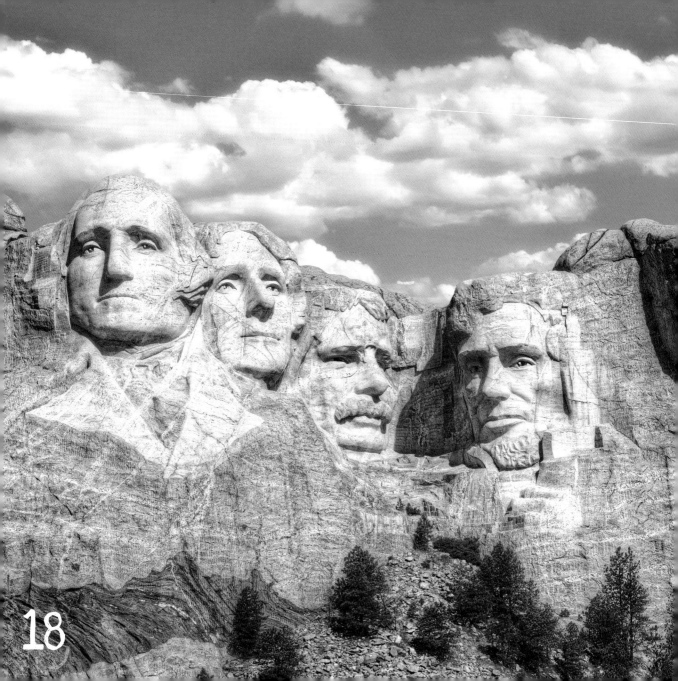

Mount Rushmore shows four American presidents. It is in South Dakota.

America has had 45 presidents since 1789!

UNITED STATES CAPITOL AT WASHINGTON.

AMERICAN PRESIDENTS. FIRST HUNDRED YEARS.
1775   1875

21

22

How do you celebrate
Presidents' Day?

Words to Know

Lincoln Memorial

Washington Monument

White House

Index

Websites

Due to the changing nature of Internet links, PowerKids Press has developed an online list of websites related to the subject of this book. This site is updated regularly. Please use this link to access the list: www.powerkidslinks.com/ushol/pres